THE HERO CODE

Also by Admiral William H. McRaven

Make Your Bed: Little Things That Can Change Your Life . . . and Maybe the World

Sea Stories: My Life in Special Operations

ADMIRAL
WILLIAM H. McRAVEN
(U.S. Navy Retired)

THE
HERO
CODE

LESSONS LEARNED FROM
LIVES WELL LIVED

GRAND CENTRAL
PUBLISHING

New York   Boston

Grand Central Publishing
Hachette Book Group
1290 Avenue of the Americas, New York, NY 10104
grandcentralpublishing.com
twitter.com/grandcentralpub

First Edition: April 2021

Grand Central Publishing is a division of Hachette Book Group, Inc. The Grand Central Publishing name and logo is a trademark of Hachette Book Group, Inc.

The publisher is not responsible for websites (or their content) that are not owned by the publisher.

The quotations used in the chapter-opening epigraphs are commonly attributed to the credited authors. In some cases, we could not confirm their original source.

The Hachette Speakers Bureau provides a wide range of authors for speaking events. To find out more, go to www.hachettespeakersbureau.com or call (866) 376-6591.

LCCN: 2020035450

ISBNs: 978-1-5387-1996-1 (hardcover), 978-1-5387-1997-8 (ebook), 978-1-5387-3736-1 (signed hardcover), 978-1-5387-3738-5 (B&N signed hardcover), 978-1-5387-0605-3 (large print)

Printed in the United States of America

LSC

Printing 1, 2021

I dedicate this book to all the remarkable men and women who battled and continue to fight the COVID-19 pandemic—the scientists, the health care professionals, those who provide and deliver our goods and services, those who teach our children, and those who protect our streets. If ever there were people worthy of the title Hero, *it is you. Thank you for all you have done for the nation and the world!*

CONTENTS

"How wonderful it is that nobody need wait a single moment before starting to improve the world."

—ANNE FRANK

INTRODUCTION

In 1960, when I was five years old, my father, an Air Force officer, was stationed in Fontainebleau, France. He was assigned to the Supreme Headquarters Allied Powers Europe (SHAPE). We lived in an old three-story home in a remote area called Bella Woods. With few modern amenities in the house and no television, I grew up devouring American comic books: Batman, Spider-Man, the Fantastic Four, the X-Men, the Hulk, Thor, and Aquaman. But there was one hero who really captured my imagination. He was all-American. His costume was red, white, and blue. He hailed from a small town in Kansas and he had amazing powers. Faster than a speeding bullet, able to leap tall buildings in a single bound, he was always rescuing women, children, and men in distress. He was "the champion of the helpless and oppressed." During the war, my hero fought the Nazis, the Fascists, the Imperial warlords, and the fifth columnists. Partnering with American soldiers and sailors, he "ventured forth in a gigantic battle for the future of Democracy," and he won. He was Action Comics Man of Steel, Superman!

I so wanted to be like Superman. There was not a towel in the house that at one point wasn't a cape. I would jump from chairs, couches, tables, anything to emulate my hero. Someday when the world was in trouble again, I knew that Superman would come to the rescue. Maybe he and I could team up. Batman had Robin; why couldn't Superman have a sidekick?

In 1963, my father received orders back to the States. My family and I traveled to Calais, France, boarded the ocean liner SS *United States*, and after a four-day trip pulled portside in New York City. No sooner had we checked in to the hotel than I turned on the television. There in amazing black and white was my hero, leaping from building to building, bullets bouncing off him, saving Lois Lane—and all this was happening in the city of Metropolis. Metropolis, New York City. I was here in Metropolis. If I was here, then maybe, just maybe, Superman was here as well.

Over the course of the next few days, my father and I explored the city. We went everywhere—the Empire State Building, the World's Fair, Times Square. But as we ventured through the canyons of skyscrapers I was constantly looking upward, hoping to catch a glimpse of the Man of Steel. My father would stop occasionally and ask me if everything was all right. *Sure, sure, everything's fine.* I mean, I was eight years old, way too old to really believe in Superman. In my mind, I knew he was just a comic book character, but in my heart, oh in my heart, I truly hoped that he was real. *Because, if Superman was real, then he could solve all of the world's problems*. Nothing was too difficult for Superman. The Nazis couldn't stop him. Aliens couldn't hurt him. No criminal was too smart to outwit my hero.

Finally, my father stopped me and asked, "Bill, what's wrong?" I was embarrassed to tell him, but after some fatherly prodding, I finally said, "Well, New York City is Metropolis and I..." I hesitated. "I was hoping to see Superman." Dad smiled, put his arm around me, pointed to a New York police officer, and said, "Son, that's the man that protects New York City."

If you can have an epiphany at eight years old, well then, this was mine. If Superman wasn't real, then who was going to save the world? If Superman or Batman or Spider-Man weren't coming, then how would we stop the criminals, the Nazis, the Soviets, the aliens from outer space, and all the violence and destruction? The answer was clear. *It was up to us.*

Over time I became fixated on real-world heroes: astronauts striving to reach the moon, doctors creating vaccines to save millions: Civic leaders marching for the rights of the underrepresented. Political leaders forming new governments where the people had a voice. Decorated soldiers returning from Korea and then Vietnam. Sports figures who transcended the color barrier. Adventurers who were climbing higher, diving deeper, sailing farther, and exploring the unknown. Visionaries who were trying to clean the air, save the oceans, and protect the fragile ecosystems. I marveled at each of these remarkable men and women, but in the back of my mind, I knew that I was nothing like them. They were smarter, stronger, braver. They had all the attributes I lacked. They had superpowers that I just didn't possess. That's why they were heroes, and that's why they were the only people who could save the world.

But I was wrong.

In 1977, I graduated from the University of Texas at Austin and joined the Navy SEALs. Over the course of the next thirty-seven years, I traveled the world. I saw the worst of humanity: war and destruction, disease and poverty, cruelty and indifference. The world was full of problems, seemingly intractable, unsolvable, impossible problems! But also in those thirty-seven years I saw the very best of mankind. Men and women who sought peace, who rebuilt nations, who cured disease and lifted the poor from poverty. Men and women whose compassion was so deep that it made the cruelty and indifference of others pale in comparison; men and women who were from all walks of life, from every socioeconomic background, from every race, every creed, and every gender and orientation.

I came to realize that there is a hero in all of us. There is an innate code that has been there since the birth of mankind. It is written in our DNA. It is what drove the great expansion of humanity out of Africa. It summoned the explorers to cross the deserts and the seas. It helped create the great faiths. It emboldened the early scientists and philosophers. It nurtured the ill and infirm. It spoke truth to the masses. It brought order to chaos and hope to the desperate. This code is not a cipher, or a cryptograph, or a puzzle to be solved. It is a moral code, an internal code of conduct that drives the human race to explore, to nurture, to comfort, to inspire, and to laugh so that societies can flourish.

This book is about heroes and the virtues they possess. You may wonder whether you can ever be as courageous or as compassionate or as humble as the men and women in these stories. *Trust me, you can!* For some, living the Hero Code comes more naturally. But for most of us, we must learn how to bring forth these virtues. We need to see them in the lives of others and try to mirror them in ourselves. We need to build those qualities through small steps that eventually become the foundation of our character.

I hope that you will find the stories in this book and these lessons of character to be of value as you build your own life, worthy of the respect of others. The hard truth is that Superman is not coming to save the day. Each of us will have to do our part. Each of us will have to find the hero inside and bring it forth. So, grab a towel, hop on a chair, and let's take that leap!

THE HERO CODE

CHAPTER ONE

Courage

★

"Courage is rightly esteemed the first of human qualities, because it is the quality which guarantees all the rest."

—WINSTON CHURCHILL

As I walked into the large command center at my Special Operations headquarters in Tampa, a sergeant dressed in his camouflage uniform called the soldiers to attention. Everyone rose from their desks and stood tall until I sat at the head table.

"Take seats," I announced.

It was the daily command briefing, and over one hundred soldiers, sailors, airmen, Marines, and civilians were situated around the room, all prepared to provide me, the four-star admiral, some insights into the events of the previous night.

On the thirty-foot-high wall in front of me was an array of seventy-inch flat panel displays, each with vital information from our special operations around the world. In the center of the wall was a massive ten-foot-square bank of cameras and microphones that provided a videoconference capability with my commanders.

Beside me sat one of my senior enlisted soldiers. As I turned to greet him, I could tell something was wrong. He was quiet and returned my greeting with a simple nod.

At the front of the command center, a young officer began to brief the results of last night's missions. He rattled off a few Ranger and SEAL operations from Afghanistan, talked about some training programs in Africa, and then came to the casualty report. I quietly said a prayer as the officer began to talk.

"Sir, last night in Kandahar province we had three soldiers killed: PFC Christopher Horns, Sergeant First Class Kris Domeij, and..." He paused. "Lieutenant Ashley White from the Cultural Support Team."

I took a deep breath.

"What happened?" I asked solemnly.

"Sir, the Rangers were conducting a routine mission in Kandahar and the Taliban compound was booby-trapped. The two Rangers and Lieutenant White stepped on a pressure plate mine and it exploded. The Rangers were killed instantly." The young officer paused again, struggling with the next sentence.

"Lieutenant White was seriously injured in the blast." He hesitated. "The medevac flew her to Kandahar, but she died at the hospital."

Everyone in the room was either looking down or looking at me.

Losing soldiers is never easy. The lives of the two Rangers were just as precious, but somehow, the father in me, the father of a daughter about Ashley's age, had a tough time accepting her loss. It was not the first female I had lost in combat, but this time it was personal. Ashley White would never have been on that mission—if not for me.

In 2008, as a three-star admiral, I took charge

of the Joint Special Operations Command. While the command was based in North Carolina, we spent most of our time in Iraq and Afghanistan. After watching our combat operations night after night, it became clear to me that we needed to have American women on our missions. We needed those women in order to engage with the Afghan females on target. The fact was, men, even Afghan men, were culturally unsuited to interact with members of the opposite sex. And yet it was the Afghan wives, the daughters, the sisters who had vital intelligence regarding the enemy we were tracking. Without female soldiers to interact with the Afghan women, we were fighting with one hand tied behind our backs. Without female soldiers, the missions were at much greater risk. But I didn't need just any female soldiers, I needed the best! I needed women who were fearless, physically and mentally tough, able to withstand the constant stress that came with war. Women who could stand side by side with combat-hardened warriors and not be intimidated by their experience, not be thrown off by their gruffness and their callous behavior. We were in hard combat every single night, and over the years the losses had mounted, and with those losses came men who were scarred by the killing. I needed women who were resilient, courageous, and fully committed to the mission. Consequently, I requested that my higher headquarters establish the female Cultural Support Teams (CSTs) to be part of my combat operations. Ashley White was one of the early volunteers.

Each CST candidate was sent to Fort Bragg, North Carolina, where they underwent extensive physical and psychological training in preparation for going overseas. Ashley was incredibly fit, able to knock out twenty pull-ups in a row and match the men on most of the physical tests. One instructor called her "the Megatron Quiet Blonde." But not only was she remarkably tough, she was a lady in every respect. Her CST teammate, Captain Meghan Curran, said that Ashley "was a wife and a daughter...she had a soft side and wasn't afraid. She wasn't afraid to be feminine and a warrior at the same time."

By August 2011, Ashley was in Afghanistan conducting missions with the 75th Ranger Regiment, the nation's most elite infantry unit. Within weeks of arriving in-country, she was engaged in a firefight with the Taliban. It earned her the coveted Combat Action Badge, given only to soldiers who had been shot at by the enemy. With her typical humility, she had dismissed the action as no big deal.

Each evening, Ashley threw on her body armor, grabbed her gun, stepped on a helicopter, and flew into the darkness of the night not knowing whether she would return. But in spite of the danger, in spite of the risks, in spite of the possibility of losing everything, her biggest fear was disappointing her fellow soldiers: not being there when they needed her. But Ashley White was *always* there for her fellow soldiers. She was *always* ready. *Always* prepared. *Always* focused on the mission. The evening of October 22, 2011, was no different. She strapped on her kit. She put aside her fears and boarded the helicopter; because no matter what the night would bring, she wasn't going to let down the soldiers she loved. The only difference this night is that Ashley's remarkable courage would cost her her life.

Combat has a way of wearing you down. The fear eats at you every night. It whispers in your ear and plays on your worst nightmares. It takes remarkable courage just to get up in the morning and face the day. It takes even greater courage to face the day with enthusiasm, knowing the challenges and the risks that confront you. But real heroes, like Ashley White, do it because they found the courage to face their fears, and that courage steels their nerves and strengthens their resolve.

In every letter I wrote to the parents or spouse of a fallen soldier, I said, without hesitation, that their heroes died doing what they loved beside men and women who loved and respected them. As painful as I knew those words might be in their time of grief, it was true. Ashley White loved the soldiers she served with, and her courage was the embodiment of that love. Just as it was with Medal of Honor recipients Lieutenant Mike Murphy, Chief Mike Monsoor, Sergeants John Chapman and Robbie Miller—or the SEALs and soldiers aboard helicopters Turbine 33 and Extortion 17 who flew to rescue their fellow warriors but never returned. Or the thousands of other soldiers, sailors, airmen, Marines, and civilians who gave so much since 9/11.

But courage is not the sole purview of warriors. Far from it. I have seen equal acts of heroism from doctors caring for the infirm, police patrolling the streets, firefighters rushing into collapsing buildings, parents protecting their children, and countless other men and women who found the courage to overcome their fears and do extraordinary things.

Sometimes, however, the physical courage to face the enemies of the nation or the threats on the street pales in comparison to the courage necessary to take on the enemy within. Each of us must deal with challenges in our lives: fear, uncertainty, regret, alcohol, drugs, depression...life. I have so often been inspired by the courage of others to face their own demons. I watched with great pride as my command sergeant major, Chris Faris, and his wife, Lisa, shared their personal story with thousands of soldiers. It was a story of Chris's post-traumatic stress and the couple's struggle to keep their family together. By coming forward, Chris and Lisa encouraged hundreds of other struggling warriors to seek help. Their courage undoubtedly saved the lives of many young men and women on the brink of suicide.

But it's not just the troops who have battled with these invisible wounds. Carter Ham, a four-star general, took the extraordinary step of going public about his battle with depression and post-traumatic stress, hoping that his revelation would encourage others to come forth. Admiral Sandy Winnefeld, the former vice chairman of the Joint Chiefs of Staff, lost a son to the opioid crisis. He and his wife, Mary, started a campaign, SAFE Project, to help others battling this addiction.

None of us are immune from life's pain and disappointment. But if you doubt for even a second that you have the courage necessary to confront the evil in the world or that weakness that resides deep inside all of us—you're wrong.

———

Legend has it that during the battle for Texas independence, Colonel William B. Travis pulled out his saber and drew a line in the sand at the feet of the men defending the Alamo. He told the men that their death at the hands of Mexican general Santa Anna's army was almost certain. Any man wishing to leave the fort could do so. But those who wanted to stay and fight should take one step forward: one step over the line in the sand. While politicians, historians, and well-meaning people on both sides may debate the righteousness of the battle, no one can dispute the courage of the men who stayed and their impact on the future of America.

We all have our lines in the sand, those fears that keep us from being courageous. But all you have to do to overcome those fears, those obstacles, those challenges in your life is to take one step forward. *Just one.* Take one step forward and get on the helicopter. Take one step forward and talk to a doctor. Take one step forward and fight injustice. Take one step forward and challenge the bullies. Take one step forward and face your inner demons. And if you take that one step forward you will find the courage you seek, the courage necessary to overcome your fears and be the hero you long to be.

The Hero Code

I will always strive to be courageous;
to take one step forward as
I confront my fears.

CHAPTER TWO

Humility

"An able yet humble man is a jewel worth a kingdom."

—WILLIAM PENN

The dining room was small and intimate, with beautiful hardwood floors and French doors that led down a wide carpeted stairway to the foyer. The head table was set for nine, and six other round tables were situated throughout the room. My host for this private dinner was Dr. Kenneth Cooper, the famed exercise cardiologist whose first book, *Aerobics*, published in 1968, inspired the fitness revolution. Dr. Cooper had invited me to speak later that evening at his Cooper Institute in Dallas. He and his wife, Millie, sat across from me. To my right were Roger Staubach, the Hall of Fame quarterback of the Dallas Cowboys, and his wife, Marianne. After my retirement from the Navy in 2014, Roger and I had become good friends. Another very nice Dallas couple was seated next to the Coopers, and to my left were an older gentleman and his wife.

Dr. Cooper made some opening remarks to his guests and then dinner was served. The Dallas couple were a bit too far away to talk with, and the Staubachs were engaged with the Coopers, so I turned my attention to the older gentleman seated closest to me. Earlier I had walked around the table introducing myself to my dinner companions, but I had failed to catch the older man's last name. I just knew he went by Charlie.

"Do you live here in Dallas?" I asked.

"No, no," he replied. "My wife, Dotty, and I live in New Braunfels."

New Braunfels was a lovely town not far from where I grew up in San Antonio.

"How'd you end up in New Braunfels?"

"Well, I was in the Air Force for a few years, and when I retired, we decided to settle in New Braunfels."

"The Air Force." I smiled. Now we had a

connection. "My father was in the Air Force, a fighter pilot, and my son is currently in the Air Force."

"Oh, I loved my time in the service," he said.

"What did you do in the Air Force?"

"I was a pilot," he replied.

Now that I looked at him, it seemed to fit. Although I would guess he was in his early eighties, he was still lean and athletic-looking and had the poise of a man who knew his worth.

"What did you fly?" I asked.

"Oh, a little bit of this and a little bit of that."

"A man of many talents, huh?"

"Or a guy who couldn't keep a job." He laughed.

I smiled at his comment, but now I was a bit hesitant to continue the discussion. Pilots can often be sensitive about where they are in the aviator pecking order, and if he wasn't at the top of the heap, the conversation could get awkward.

Over the course of the evening, I extracted a bit more information from my new acquaintance, but in general, Charlie seemed very reluctant to talk about himself. He was much more interested in me and my family. He wanted to know all about my son in the Air Force and my other two children. He was so very impressed that my wife and I were celebrating our fortieth wedding anniversary, even though it was clear to me that his wife, Dotty, was the love of his life, and they had been married quite a bit longer. He asked about my career in the Navy, and as it turned out, Charlie had attended the Naval Academy before transferring to the Air Force.

By the time dessert arrived, I felt like we were good friends. His quiet confidence, gentle nature, and genuine interest in me and my family built an instant rapport that often takes years to develop. He also reminded me a lot of my father. He smiled often, laughed with ease, and was so very gracious to everyone at the table. However, in our hour of dining, I still hadn't caught his full name. As we broke from the dinner table, I rose and thanked Charlie and Dotty for a wonderful evening. They extended an invitation for Georgeann and me to come to New Braunfels sometime and join them for a barbecue. It was a trip I hoped to make someday.

As we walked down the stairway to the foyer, Roger Staubach pulled up alongside me.

"Sounds like you and Charlie were having a great conversation," he said.

"Yeah, what a wonderful guy," I responded.

"Can you imagine what it must have been like?" Staubach said.

"What do you mean?" I asked.

"I mean, walking on the moon. Think of it. Only twelve men in the history of the world have done that."

"I'm sorry, Roger, what are you talking about?"

"Charlie. Charlie Duke," he said.

"What about Charlie Duke?"

Roger laughed. "You didn't know?"

"Know what?" I asked.

"Charlie Duke was the youngest man ever to walk on the moon."

I dropped my head in embarrassment. Of course! *General Charles Duke*, United States Air Force, the tenth man and still youngest ever to set foot on the surface of the moon. After graduating from the Naval Academy in 1957, Duke transferred to the Air Force and became a test pilot. In 1966 he was accepted into the astronaut program. Duke was the voice of Mission Control during Apollo 11's first moon landing. As the backup crew on the ill-fated Apollo 13, Duke and fellow astronauts John Young and Ken Mattingly worked in the simulator to find a solution to bring the crew home safely. Then on April 16, 1972, Duke and Young landed in the Descartes Highlands, the highest point on the moon, and subsequently conducted three rover missions to survey the surrounding area.

"You know," I said, turning to Roger, "during our entire dinner conversation, never once did he mention the small, trivial, insignificant fact...*that he walked on the moon!*"

"I'm not surprised." Roger smiled. "He's a very humble man."

As I found out later, though, Charlie Duke's humility was hard won. After the moon landing, he was a national hero. The allure of fame and fortune put a great deal of stress on his marriage and his family. All that changed, though, when Dotty became a Christian and Charlie soon followed. Their Christian faith taught them humility and helped them recognize that in the vastness of the universe, in the incalculable complexity of nature, in the epic story of human evolution, our greatest individual accomplishments, *even walking on the moon*, pale in comparison to God's works. In Matthew 23:12, Jesus says, "Whoever exalts himself will be humbled, and whoever humbles himself will be exalted."

But it is not just Christianity that extols the virtues of humility. The Quran tells us that "the servants of the most merciful are those who walk upon the Earth in humility." In the Old Testament,

Proverbs 11:2 says, "...with humility comes wisdom." Confucius offers that "humility is the solid foundation of all virtues." Hindus believe that "only the humble know how to appreciate and admire the good qualities of others," and the Buddha says, "You learn nothing from life if you think you are right all the time." Even the Greek philosopher Socrates boldly exclaimed that he was the *wisest man in Greece*, because he knew that compared to God, "the wisdom of men is worth little or nothing."

Humility is the simplest of all heroic qualities to assume, and yet the least expressed. To be humble is to recognize that one's intellect, one's physical strengths, one's wealth all pale when compared to the vastness, the complexity, the richness, the power, and the grandeur of the universe. And if we are humbled by our place in the universe, then we are much more likely to see that our differences are infinitely small. We are much more likely to see that our understanding is equally fraught and that our power to overcome even the tiniest challenges is similarly difficult. Humility is born of respect. Respect for what we do not know. Respect for what we cannot readily see. But out of this humble approach to life, we are more likely to appreciate the beauty that surrounds us, more likely to gaze into a microscope or peer at the stars and be awed, more likely to be inspired by little acts of kindness. And we are much more likely to treat others as we would have them treat us.

The power of humility is that it brings us closer together, and the role of every hero is to unite people, not divide them. *Be humble. It will serve you well.*

The Hero Code

I will work to be humble; to recognize the limits of my intellect, my understanding, and my power.

CHAPTER THREE

Sacrifice

"He who would accomplish little must sacrifice little; he who would achieve much must sacrifice much; he who would attain highly must sacrifice greatly."

—JAMES ALLEN

I sat silently as the man on the small stage began to speak. Dressed in a sport coat and slacks, he was tall, fit, and had the military bearing that marked him as a former Marine. In his mid-seventies, retired lieutenant Patrick "Clebe" McClary, USMC, had a thick southern accent and was a bit sunburned on his pale bald head. I remember thinking that were it not for his missing arm and the black patch over his left eye, he likely could be serving today. But as McClary was quick to point out, he wouldn't be here today were it not for the sacrifice of a young black Marine on a hill in Vietnam in 1968, an act of heroism that would change so many lives and give an entire generation a new perspective on human dignity.

———

The sun had long set atop Hill 146 in the Quan Duc Valley of Vietnam when the small fifteen-man reconnaissance team landed. Disembarking from the helo, McClary, the officer in charge, immediately ordered his men to fan out and take up fighting positions. The hill, or what was left of it, was covered with mines, booby traps, and the insidious punji pits, deep holes filled with poison-tipped stakes. Hill 146 was a strategic position in the valley; the Marines knew it, and so did the North Vietnamese Army.

Over the course of the next day, this recon element of Marines, known by their call sign, Texas Pete, continued to reinforce their foxholes and pre-pare for a possible enemy attack.

Just as the dawn was breaking on March 5, 1968, rockets began raining in from a large North Vietnamese and Vietcong force. Up from the val-ley, enemy sappers, with grenades and demolition charges strapped to their chest, began a suicide charge. McClary, barking orders and calling for artillery support, ran from foxhole to foxhole as the Vietcong began a full-on assault.

From their position on the edge of the hill, Private First Class Ralph Johnson and two fellow Marines began to engage the enemy. All around their foxhole, "satchel charges," canvas bags filled with explosives, were being tossed by the advancing Vietcong. Large-caliber rounds whizzed by their heads, and the noise from the explosions was deafening. Before long, the overwhelming enemy force was converging on their position.

"Grenade!" someone yelled in the distance, and the three Marines instinctively hit the dirt. The ground erupted a few yards away. "Grenade!" came the call again and another one exploded, this time even closer. The Vietcong were advancing quickly now, and Johnson and the other two Marines were running low on ammunition.

McClary, having been rocked by one of the explosions, dove for the closest foxhole, within feet of Ralph Johnson. As Johnson and his fellow recon

Marines continued to fire at the charging Vietcong, an enemy grenade landed with a dull thud at the heel of Johnson's boot.

"Grenade!" Johnson yelled, and without hesitation, the nineteen-year-old Marine smothered the explosive with his body, shielding his fellow warriors from the blast. The grenade ripped through Ralph Johnson, killing him instantly. Stunned by their loss and inspired by Johnson's remarkable heroism, the Texas Pete Marines rallied against the Vietcong and held on until reinforcements arrived.

An isolated hillside in the middle of Vietnam seemed an unlikely place to change America. But after the battle for Hill 146, the news of Ralph Johnson's sacrifice spread quickly. This young black Marine, raised in the Deep South, with little formal education, living under Jim Crow, gave his last full measure of devotion to the men he served with.

After Clebe McClary recovered from his wounds and more than thirty operations, he would make it his calling in life to tell the story of Ralph Johnson and his fellow Marines. Men and women of all ages and colors would hear how this humble young man from Charleston lived the scripture of John 15:13 and laid down his life for his friends.

For his actions that day, Private First Class Ralph H. Johnson would receive the Medal of Honor, posthumously. But his sacrifice would result in more than just the nation's highest honor. It would open the eyes of so many Americans, who, caught up in the racial strife of the 1960s, would see this unselfish act, this split-second decision to save his fellow Marines, as an inspiration to all, as a recognition that we are all worthy of respect and sacrifice, regardless of color.

———

March 28, 2018, was a cold day in Charleston. I came to attention and placed my hand over my heart as the Marine color guard presented the colors and the band played the national anthem. Before me alongside the pier was the newest destroyer in the

United States Navy, the USS *Ralph Johnson*. Over five thousand people were in attendance, including the extended Johnson family and Ralph's sister Helen.

The crew of the *Ralph Johnson*, dressed in immaculate blue uniforms, "brought the ship to life," running to their combat stations and coming to attention. As the cold spring wind whipped down the pier, the dignitaries, from the former governor of South Carolina to the commandant of the Marine Corps, began their speeches. It was hard not to smile, to see the changes, to feel the respect, to know that we were a better nation because of Ralph Johnson.

In his remarks, Senator Tim Scott, the first African American senator from the state of South Carolina, said that Ralph Johnson "began a legacy that should last an eternity. He had a vision that we should all embrace—that we are better together. He was willing to sacrifice his life for a cause greater than himself. It is the essence of service over self. Our true heroes come from obscurity, but they will live eternally in our hearts and our minds and hopefully in our actions."

Ralph Johnson was willing to sacrifice his life for a noble cause: not the Vietnam War, but the love and friendship of the men who served with him. That one brief act of heroism on a hill far, far away changed forever the lives of his fellow Marines and left a legacy that will last an eternity.

For most of us, however, our sacrifices do not come in one shining moment of extraordinary valor. For most of us, our sacrifices are little acts of giving that build upon themselves and over time become something worthwhile, something remarkable: the single mother who works two jobs to care for her children; the teacher who labors over a struggling student; the cop who coaches youth basketball; the child who nurses their ailing parent. What makes these sacrifices so heroic is that there are no adoring crowds to thank you, no awards to receive, and no gilded words about your bravery. Nothing accrues to you but the knowledge that your actions were noble—an act of grace with no expectation of gratitude.

All of these sacrifices are an investment in humanity, and like any investment, adding a little every day will make you wealthy. Not the kind of wealth you can spend, but the kind of wealth that will make you rich—rich in gratitude, rich in satisfaction, rich in appreciation.

Learning to sacrifice is easy. Start by *giving a little of yourself, every day*. Give a little time to your friends. Give a little of your treasure to a worthy cause. Give a little love to your family. Every day—without fail—*give a little of yourself*. The giving will become a habit, a part of your character. In a month, in a year, in a decade, in a lifetime, all that sacrifice will add up to something special. If you do this, the sacrifice will be a blessing, a reward, a magnificent obsession, and no burden will be too great—and you will leave behind a legacy worthy of respect and admiration. A hero.

The Hero Code

I will learn to sacrifice by giving
a little of my time, my talent,
and my treasure to those in need.
Every day. Without fail.

CHAPTER FOUR

Integrity

"The supreme quality of leadership is unquestionably integrity; without it no real success is possible, no matter whether it is on a section gang, a football field, in an army, or in an office."

—DWIGHT D. EISENHOWER

Not all important lessons in my life were learned on the battlefield...

As I hurried down the long corridor of the Pentagon, reams of paper tucked under my arm, I tried not to look too anxious. It was my first day on a new assignment. I was headed to a meeting on the fabled "E" Ring where all the powerful men and women in the building had their offices—the secretary of defense, the chairman and vice chairman of the Joint Chiefs, all the four-star admirals and generals—the place where decisions that affected the fate of the world were made.

Dressed in my summer white Navy uniform, I walked confidently past a senior officer, who smiled and nodded, as though he remembered the time when he was a young lieutenant, fresh-faced and eager to make a difference.

Stopping periodically to check the numbers on the door, I finally reached the conference room. Easing the door open, I peered inside, and there was my boss, Captain Ted Grabowsky.

"Good, good. Let me have those slides," he said without even looking up.

"Yes sir," I responded, handing him the stack of papers and slides I was holding.

Shuffling through the slides, he pulled out the top ten view graphs, held them up to the light, and mumbled to himself. "Good, good," he said again.

Grabowsky was not your Hollywood casting call for a Navy SEAL. Short, bespectacled, he walked with a slight limp from a glider accident and squinted when he talked. And he talked a lot. He could be gruff and demanding, but I also found him to be brilliant, insightful, hardworking, and incredibly tenacious. Somewhere along the way, I had earned his respect, and he had requested that I join him at the Pentagon.

Moments later, a crowd started gathering. Officers and civilians from around the building were there to discuss the Navy SEAL budget for the next two years. Vietnam was over and money was tight. The Cold War was in full swing and many questioned the need for the Navy's commandos. Without a strong budget, without money to train and build modern facilities, our future looked dire.

Once everyone was seated, we waited for the arrival of the big guy.

"Attention on deck!" came the call as the admiral entered the room.

"At ease," he said immediately.

Vice Admiral Joe Metcalf was the quintessential salty admiral. His reputation as a tough, cigar-smoking, hard-nosed, no-nonsense warrior was well earned. A Vietnam veteran who subsequently led the 1983 U.S. invasion of Grenada, he intimidated people and seemed to take great pride in doing so.

"All right, Ted," Metcalf growled, chewing on an unlit cigar. "Let's get on with this."

"Yes sir," Grabowsky responded.

As Grabowsky began the briefings, I glanced down at the spreadsheet outlining all the money we needed to keep the SEALs in business. This was going to be a tough sell. Every dollar we added to the SEAL budget took away from the fighter pilots, the ship drivers, and the submariners. At a time when Reagan was building to a six-hundred-ship Navy, no one wanted a bunch of Vietnam-era jungle fighters. If you didn't bring a nuclear-tipped bomb to the fight against the Soviets, you weren't of much value to the Pentagon.

With each slide that Grabowsky briefed, Metcalf harrumphed and rolled his eyes. Around the room, the green eyeshade guys were taking notes and shaking their heads east to west. We were losing the budget battle.

Finally, Grabowsky finished and the room grew quiet.

Having gnawed through the last inch of his cigar, the admiral stood and paced in front of the long table.

"Look, Ted," he snarled. "I want to help, but do you really need all this money?" Pulling the cigar from his mouth, he pointed the stub at the graph on the screen. "I mean, how much ammo do you SEALs shoot? What about these mini-submarines? Do you really need six of them?"

I may have been new to the Pentagon, but I understood how the resourcing game was played. As the briefer, you never, ever backed off on your numbers. The implication was that you had done everything possible to whittle the budget down to exactly what was needed, or you would never have the temerity to stand before a three-star admiral and request this much money.

Grabowsky paused momentarily.

"Sir. You're right," he said. "We can take some cuts to the ammunition line, and I'll talk to the SEAL Teams about reducing the number of mini-subs from six to three."

Around the room the green eyeshade guys seemed a bit stunned. Suddenly they were poring over the spreadsheet and conferring with each other. Metcalf glanced in their direction and they nodded their approval.

"All right," Metcalf announced. "If you can make this work, then you will live to fight another day." He laughed, shook hands with Grabowsky, and left the room. The bean counters followed after him.

We had just lost millions of dollars from our budget, but Grabowsky didn't seem fazed by it.

"Sir, I know this is my first day," I said. "But it seems like we just got clobbered."

Grabowsky smiled. "On the contrary. We just survived an L-shaped ambush, flanked the enemy, and came out the victor."

"What?"

"Look, Bill. The comptroller folks already knew that we could live without the ammo money, and they certainly expected that we could get by without three extra mini-subs. If I had objected too loudly it would have killed our credibility."

He motioned for me to take a seat.

"If you're going to survive in this building, then there is one rule you have to follow."

I leaned in closer, wanting to know the secret of the Pentagon.

"You must never lie or misrepresent the truth. If you do, you will get caught, and then you are of no value to me anymore. No one will trust you, and without trust, none of our work can get done."

He paused as he gathered up the last of the papers.

"That's my Golden Rule. Never forget it."

Over the next three years in the Pentagon and my twenty-five years in the Navy that followed, I never forgot Grabowsky's "Golden Rule": the relationship between honesty and trust. Honesty wasn't just about being morally upright; it had a value proposition. If you were honest and people trusted you, then they trusted you with the big jobs, they trusted you with their money, they trusted you with their reputation, they trusted you with their friendship, they trusted you with their family, and they trusted you with their lives. Even when they didn't like you or didn't agree with you, they knew you to be upright and trustworthy.

Honesty is the cornerstone of integrity, the foundation upon which all other aspects of your character will be built. But honesty alone is not sufficient to be a person of integrity. Integrity requires action. To be known as men and women of integrity you must demonstrate your moral backbone. You must be confronted with an ethical dilemma—a choice between one road that is rocky, steep, and treacherous and the other that is smooth, flat, and comfortable. One road tests your fortitude, the other provides an easy path. One is filled with temporary hardships and pain, the other is quick and easy. But in the end, if you choose the harder path less traveled, the path where the virtuous have walked, the journey will make you stronger, more resilient, and more capable of conquering the other steep climbs on your way to the top. While the second path, the easy way, will leave you unprepared for the future challenges of life.

————

My mother, a schoolteacher from East Texas, worked hard her whole life to shape my character. She often told me stories of great acts of integrity as examples for me to emulate. Her favorite was the account of American patriot and future president John Adams, who defended British soldiers after the Boston Massacre.

On March 5, 1770, a mob of three hundred colonists surrounded and threatened a small contingent of redcoats. As tensions escalated, the soldiers fired on the mob, killing five Americans. Bostonians were furious and threatened to lynch the soldiers for murder. A trial was ordered, but no one would take the case for fear they might be lynched along with the British.

In spite of the threats and in spite of the impact on his personal and professional reputation, John

Adams accepted the position as defense counsel. He believed that if Americans were ever going to show that they were worthy of self-rule, then the colonists must give the soldiers a fair trial. In the end, the jury found the British not guilty by reason of self-defense. The willingness of Adams to put the interests of justice above his own self-interest helped shape the American legal system and forged Adams's reputation as a man of uncompromising integrity.

The lesson of John Adams was not lost on me. Over the years, I was frequently confronted with situations where my own self-interest and preservation were in conflict with doing the right thing. I hope my mother would be proud of my choices.

Being men and women of integrity—following the rules, following the law, and following what you know to be right—is hard. It is hard because you have to fight against your natural herd tendencies: the desire to go along, to get along, to be well liked among the herd.

It is hard because unlike the comic book heroes, you are not men and women of steel, you are not cloaked in suits of armor, and you do not have unearthly powers.

It is hard because you are human, because life often forces you into seemingly untenable positions, because good and evil are always in conflict.

It is hard—and I dare say that you will fail occasionally. And when you fail to uphold your integrity, it should make you sick to your stomach. It should give you sleepless nights. You should be so tortured that you promise yourself never to do it again.

Being a hero will not be easy. And what makes real heroes are their struggles and their ability to overcome them. But no matter how mightily you might struggle, the world will believe in you, follow you, and allow themselves to be saved—if they know you to be honest, trustworthy, of good character and good faith. Never fear the path that is rocky, steep, and treacherous: There you will find men and women of integrity. *There you will find heroes.*

The Hero Code

I will be a person of integrity; every decision I make and every action I take will be moral, legal, and ethical.

CHAPTER FIVE

Compassion

---✶---

"Our human compassion binds us the one to the other—not in pity or patronizingly, but as human beings who have learnt how to turn our common suffering into hope for the future."

—NELSON MANDELA

Through the small plexiglass window, I could see the armed soldier standing guard outside our room. I knew that there was another soldier positioned at the other door and five to ten more manning key positions around the dining facility. While Bagram Air Base in Afghanistan was reasonably secure, the insider threat from a potential suicide bomber was always a possibility.

Inside the room, there were trays of food on fold-up tables situated in a long rectangle to allow the twenty generals to eat while listening to the commander of the U.S. Central Command, General John Abizaid. As the only one-star admiral in the group and one of the junior officers, I sat at the far end of the rectangle as Abizaid began to talk. It was an impromptu Commanders' Conference and we had just started to discuss the strategy for the following year. These were high-level, important, life-altering discussions that would have a dramatic effect on the future of U.S. forces in the war.

As I wolfed down my burger and ranch-style beans, I tried to keep an eye on Abizaid as he talked. A remarkable officer, Abizaid had that swagger and sense of confidence that come from being in command most of his adult life. He did not suffer fools gladly, and while his exterior demeanor was always professional, he had a lighter side that occasionally came forth. But these were serious times and Abizaid was in the middle of a serious discussion. Sitting at the head of the long table, he was pointing to various officers as each man spoke about his unit's role in the overall strategy.

Just as I was finishing off my burger, I saw the door to the room ease open and Abizaid's military aide cautiously entered. The general was in the midst of making an important point when the aide sidled up beside him. Not wanting to interrupt the general, the aide stood quietly off his right shoulder. Finally, Abizaid stopped and turned to him.

"What? What is it?"

Clearly uncomfortable with what he had to say, the aide whispered into Abizaid's ear.

"What? Now?"

"Yes sir. He's right outside," the aide responded.

"Who is this guy again?"

The aide whispered once more.

"All right. Let him in," Abizaid said, visibly annoyed.

Moments later, the door to the dining room swung open and in walked a man in civilian clothes: clearly out of place in Bagram. Surveying the room, the civilian looked stunned to see so many generals. In a bit of a panic, he blurted out, "Who's in charge here? Who can I talk to?"

Around the table the generals laughed softly. Abizaid, now with a smile on his face, said, "Well, I guess I am. What can I do for you?"

"Are you the big guy?" the civilian asked.

Once again there were a few muffled laughs.

"It depends. What do you need?"

The civilian moved to the head of the table and stood beside Abizaid. It was clear that he was uncomfortable and working hard not to show it.

"Well. I'm Gary Sinise. I'm an actor."

Everyone in the room looked at one another. They had been at war for a while, and the actor's name and face weren't ringing a lot of bells.

"I played Lieutenant Dan in the movie *Forrest Gump.*"

Now heads were nodding. *Oh yes. We know this guy. He was good in the role. Very good!*

"What can I do for you, Mr. Sinise?" Abizaid asked.

"Well, General, I need a C-130 aircraft. Can you get me one?"

A few more stifled laughs.

"Maybe," Abizaid said, a sly grin breaking across his face. "What do you need it for?"

"General, I have ten pallets of school supplies that I want to give to the children of Afghanistan, and I don't have any way of getting the pallets to them."

Abizaid's eyes widened a bit. "Where did you get these supplies?" he asked.

"I bought them, sir. It's part of an effort called Operation International Children."

"I'm sorry, Mr. Sinise, let me get this straight. You bought school supplies for the children of Afghanistan and you came all the way here to deliver them?"

Sinise looked perplexed. "Well, yes sir. The kids need the supplies. I thought I could help."

"You do know that we're in the middle of a war. This isn't exactly a safe place for a civilian."

Sinise looked around the room at the men in camouflage uniforms. "Yes sir. I know. But the kids need the school supplies or we will have an entire generation of Afghans who don't have a proper education."

The laughs in the room had turned to smiles.

"Well, I'll tell you what, Mr. Sinise. I'll see what I can do about that C-130," Abizaid said.

"Thank you, General. And I'm sorry to interrupt."

"No problem, Mr. Sinise. It was a welcome interruption."

Abizaid stood, smiled widely, and shook hands with Sinise. They took some quick photos and then Sinise departed.

As the door swung closed and Gary Sinise left, the entire tenor of the room changed.

It is easy to get jaded by war. You grow callous at the injustice, the pain, the lost lives, and the lost futures. You tell yourself that you can't weep for every dying soul; you can't hurt for the assorted wrongs in the world. So you place the discomfort of war deep inside yourself and you surround it with every emotional barricade you can. You never want those feelings of pity and disappointment to come out, because if they do, they will crush the warrior in you; they will take away your edge and your determination to defeat the enemy. But every now and then you see an act of kindness and charity that makes you long for the days when you didn't have to hide your sympathy, your mercy, or your sadness, where you could cheer for the do-gooders, smile at the little acts of humanity, and be proud of the merciful. Within hours, Gary Sinise got his C-130 and the supplies made their way to hundreds of Afghan children.

A few years later as I was visiting one of my wounded soldiers at Walter Reed, I walked into the room and there was Gary Sinise with his daughter. He had arrived, unannounced, with no fanfare, bearing gifts for a soldier he didn't know. Over the course of the next decade, everywhere I went, Gary had been there and left his mark, caring for soldiers and their families. Through his foundation and Lt. Dan Band, he has raised millions of dollars to help the wounded and the families of the fallen. What makes his actions so special is the sincerity of his giving and his unbridled compassion. Every handshake is a bond of friendship. Every hug is a promise of support. Every smile is genuine. The influence of one man and his deep wellspring of charity and goodwill changed the lives of so very many.

———

When I was a boy, my mother was always fond of telling me the story of the North Platte Canteen. North Platte was a small town in rural Nebraska, a rest stop on the Union Pacific Railroad carrying soldiers from the West Coast to the troopships heading for Europe during World War II. One day a young woman decided to make some sandwiches for the soldiers on the train. Her act of kindness was so well received that before long all of North Platte turned out to provide food, gifts, cards, letters, a dance or two, money, anything to help the soldiers on their way to war. Over the next four years, the townsfolk cared for over six million soldiers, and every soldier remembered the thoughtfulness of the people of North Platte. Imagine the effect that kindness had on the war effort.

I witnessed great acts of compassion almost daily during my time in uniform and beyond: members of the Red Cross helping the victims of the 2008 earthquake in Pakistan and the 2013 typhoon that leveled the Philippines; doctors volunteering their time to care for the wounded in Yemen; charity groups providing food to the destitute in the Congo; neighbors holding vigils for fallen heroes across America; passengers cheering the arrival of an Honor Flight in Washington; a thousand acts of kindness from soldiers to Afghan and Iraqi villagers; people of every social status, color, and creed helping others during the devastation of Hurricane Harvey—all acts, great or small, meant to convey our common humanity, a recognition that we are all worthy of some respect, some outpouring of love.

Science tells us that certain acts of giving cause the brain to secrete a hormone that generates feelings of well-being. But we don't really need science to tell us that doing charitable acts makes us feel good about ourselves. Since childhood, most of us have known that "it is better to give than to receive." But why? Why? Because…it is embedded in our humanity. The fact is, no society can long survive unless there exist strong bonds between individuals, families, communities, states, and nations: neighbors helping neighbors, communities coming together in times of need, each act strengthening the fabric of society, and by doing so, allowing for the survival of the species. If we lose our sense of charity, of kindness, of compassion, if we become hardened to the troubles of others, then we will not survive long.

For some the desire to give is strong. They feel the pain of others. They have empathy for the lost and unfortunate. They are naturally caring people. We all know someone like that. But most of us must search for the desire to be kind. Life can make us selfish, skew our priorities toward work, wealth, and image. Our character, the qualities that make us most human, most able to fit well into society, can be diminished by the trappings of modernity. Fortunately, the fix is easy: one dollar for the homeless, one hour at a soup kitchen, one dinner for the church bazaar, one thank-you for the returning soldiers, one small act of kindness to forge your character, strengthen your soul, and keep you connected to the rest of the world.

The Hero Code

I will be kind and compassionate
to at least one person every single day
and expect nothing in return.

CHAPTER SIX

Perseverance

---✶---

"I have never had to face anything that could overwhelm the native optimism and stubborn perseverance I was blessed with."

—JUSTICE SONIA SOTOMAYOR

The man in the rumpled white lab coat looked like an Einsteinian character out of central casting. His long gray hair was unkempt, he hadn't shaved in several days, and he had that faraway look that told me he was thinking deeply about something important.

"Jim, Jim," I said, trying to break his concentration.

Hearing my voice, he smiled and reached out his hand.

"Oh, Chancellor. Good to see you. How have you been?"

Dr. Jim Allison always seemed to be in a good mood and always seemed to be ruminating about the next great breakthrough in science. As we stood in the ballroom of the hotel waiting for Allison to give a lunchtime presentation, I leaned in close so others around us couldn't hear.

"Well, Jim, I've got some bad news." I paused. "I received word from the *Dallas Morning News* that they chose someone else as their 2015 Texan of the Year. I'm really sorry. After all you have accomplished in medicine, I thought you clearly deserved it."

"Oh, don't be sorry!" he said. "Your nominating letter was great. And guess what!" Allison smiled like a teenager with a new car. "Willie Nelson's band called me. They saw your letter in the paper and the part about me playing the harmonica."

The smile got even bigger.

"They have invited me to go onstage and play with them."

"That's fantastic!" I said.

"Yeah, but I have to tell you, Chancellor. I'm really nervous. I mean, this is Willie Nelson!"

Inside I couldn't help but laugh. *This is Willie*

Nelson? Well, Willie, I thought, *this is Jim Allison, and he's saving the world from cancer.*

———

James Patrick Allison was born in Alice, Texas, in 1948. A rambunctious kid with two older brothers, he was always getting into teenager trouble. He was hardheaded and loved to challenge authority. His father was a country doctor and on the road a lot. His mother was a loving housewife and a great caregiver to the boys. Tragically, she died of lymphoma when Jim was just eleven. Later, her two brothers would also die of cancer. As devastating as those losses were, they spurred Jim Allison on his long quest to find a cure for cancer.

Graduating from high school at the age of sixteen, Allison went on to the University of Texas at Austin. He was not your typical science geek. Jim loved to party at the local honky-tonks and play his ever-present harmonica. But science was his passion. When he wasn't partying, he was in the lab. In the labs at the University of Texas, he first studied T-cells, the cells in the human body that attack and kill viruses. It occurred to him that the human immune system could be used to fight cancer. For years he pursued this radical idea, studying and researching every aspect of the immune system and its effect on tumors. He was so enthralled by the prospect that he wrote his doctoral thesis on how bacteria help boost the immune system in its fight against childhood leukemia. This concept of using the immune system to attack cancer was considered by most physicians to be a fool's errand. But Allison persisted.

"The number one thing I learned in the lab, which is how important it is just to persevere. Not being so disappointed...Just keep working." It was an attitude that would define the rest of his career.

After receiving his PhD in 1973, Allison headed off to Scripps Clinic in California, and then in 1977 returned to Texas to work at MD Anderson Cancer

Center. While there, he continued to focus on the T-cell as a possible means to attack cancer cells.

In 1985, Allison moved to Berkeley, California, where his research determined that T-cells had a receptor on them. This receptor was like a flange or an arm that, when connected to a healthy cell, acted as a "braking mechanism," preventing the T-cell from killing it. But the insidious cancer cells knew exactly where that receptor was located, and they were able to trick the immune system into thinking they were benign. Allison believed that if he could prevent the cancer from sealing off the receptor (with an antibody), then the T-cells could identify the cancer as malignant and destroy it. The key was finding a way to control the braking mechanism so that the T-cells could fight the bad cancer and not kill the good cells.

In 1995, Allison injected a dozen mice with cancer tumors and then gave them the antibody that he hoped would prevent the cancer from blocking the T-cell receptor. When he checked on the mice several days later, their tumors had unfortunately grown larger. Dismayed by the results, he assumed his experiment had failed. But just two days after his initial examination, almost all the tumors had vanished. The results were considered impossible! His colleagues were stunned by the data. Never before had anyone seen such dramatic improvement in so little time.

Surely the research community would rise up now and embrace these new developments. It wouldn't be long before a lifesaving therapeutic could be available to help those with cancer. Surely. Surely...

Surely not.

For the next fifteen years, Jim Allison fought to bring his discovery to the world. The research community was not as enthusiastic as he had hoped. All previous attempts to use the human immune system to cure cancer had been only marginally successful. Many believed that Allison's science was "a bunch of voodoo." Additionally, the big pharmaceutical companies had been burned by an array of drugs that took hundreds of millions of dollars and years to develop, only to be of limited success. Everywhere Jim Allison went he was told no. *No, we will not provide you with funding. No, we will not invest years in clinical trials. No, we don't think the science is strong enough. And what don't you understand about no?* But Allison believed in the science.

Jim was obsessed with getting his treatment to market. "I think any great big disruptive change that you're pushing for is going to take some single-mindedness," he said. That dogged persistence, that ability to persevere through every challenge he confronted, was the difference between success and failure.

Finally, after he had struggled for years to get support, Bristol Myers Squibb agreed to fund human trials. One of Dr. Allison's early clinical trials was on a young woman of twenty-three who had been battling metastatic melanoma. The cancer had spread to her liver and her brain. Prior to the clinical trial, she had undergone three different forms of chemo-therapy and radiation for a brain tumor. Nothing worked. Her body was failing and her prognosis was grim. In 2006, she was given Allison's experimental drug. Within days she began to feel better, and within a week her brain scan revealed that the tumor was gone. *Completely vanished!* Fourteen years later she remains cancer free.

In 2011, the FDA approved Allison's drug ipili-mumab (ipi) for use in fighting cancer. Since that time over one million patients have received the drug, and while it hasn't cured everyone, hundreds of thousands of people are alive today because Jim Allison refused to give up.

Let me repeat that last bit: *Hundreds of thousands of people are alive today!* His perseverance paid off.

In 2017, Jim Allison walked onto the stage at the Austin City Limits music festival, pulled a harmonica from his back pocket, and joined Willie Nelson in playing "Roll Me Up and Smoke Me When I Die." Twelve months later he walked onto another stage in Stockholm, Sweden, where he received the Nobel Prize in Medicine.

I believe history will show that success is not just a function of brains or brawn, of talent or intellect, of skill or resourcefulness, but of perseverance. Genius without resolve is just another passing person with a bright idea. Athletic prowess without determination is just another talent wasted. The world is filled with men and women who amounted to nothing because they gave up on their dreams: because they didn't have the guts, the determination, the willpower to keep going—no matter what. But history is equally replete with heroes who fought through the challenges, persevered, and made a difference.

George Washington was defeated on the battlefield more times than he won. Abraham Lincoln lost eight elections before he won the presidency. Thomas Edison failed ten thousand times before inventing the lightbulb. Henry Ford had two failed companies before he found success. J. K. Rowling was destitute before she got the first Harry Potter book published, and Oprah Winfrey had an extremely difficult childhood before finding her way. Martin Luther King once famously said, "If you can't fly, run. If you can't run, walk. If you can't walk, crawl. But by all means, keep moving."

———

I am often asked about what it takes to get through Navy SEAL training. Many young sailors think it's about the number of push-ups you can do or how fast you can run or improving your swim time. It is none of those things. I have seen the finest athletes in the nation drop out after the first week, and conversely, I have seen young men with just a little talent excel in training. The answer is simple. To get through SEAL training, you just don't quit. Period. That's it.

So how do you persevere? We have a saying in SEAL training: "Take it one evolution at a time." As prospective "frogmen," we start off as "tadpoles" in training and must *evolve* to reach our goal. These evolutions are individual events: long runs, open-ocean swims, hours of physical training, each accompanied by pain, exhaustion, and frequent failure. The student who looks too far into the future often fears that he will have to endure more than he is able. If he sees the future as a never-ending series of obstacles, then the challenges sometimes seem too daunting to overcome. However, if you take each hurdle as it comes, not worrying about the next event, the next day, the next month, or the next year, then before long one hurdle cleared becomes two, and two becomes three, and just like that, the task is finished.

Life can be complicated at times. But the challenges you face are the same ones that billions of people have encountered throughout history. Those who have conquered the obstacles before them, whether personal or professional, have one thing in common. They never gave up. *Neither should you!*

The Hero Code

I will never give up on matters
that are important to me, my family,
my country, or my faith.
I will persevere.

CHAPTER SEVEN

Duty

"I long to accomplish a great and noble task, but it is my chief duty to accomplish small tasks as if they were great and noble."

—HELEN KELLER

The heavy brass plaque on the outside of the office read *Senator John McCain, Arizona*. I tugged on the coat of my Navy dress blue uniform, straightened my tie, and opened the door. Inside, a young man sitting behind a desk greeted me. He asked me to have a seat while he informed the senator of my arrival. I sat down on one of the three chairs in the small outer office.

McCain was my first visit of the day. I had been recommended for promotion to four-star admiral and assignment as the commander of the United States Special Operations Command. But before any of that could happen, the Senate had to confirm my appointment. This meant a confirmation hearing. Prior to the hearing, I was to meet with key senators so they could "get to know me."

Moments later, McCain entered the room. With

a big smile on his face and a hearty handshake, he welcomed me into his office. As we sat around his coffee table, I couldn't help but gaze at some of his memorabilia: pictures with various world leaders, newspaper articles citing his leadership, magazines with his face on the cover, and a host of Navy collectibles from various ships and submarines. Tucked in the corner behind his desk was a picture of a young Lieutenant Commander John McCain. It gave me pause. I knew that the man sitting across from me was more than just a U.S. senator. He was an American hero, the embodiment of duty to his country.

———

Senator John McCain was the son and grandson of Navy four-star admirals. His grandfather, John S. McCain Sr., commanded carrier task forces during some of the most historic operations in World War II. His father, John S. McCain Jr., became the commander in chief of the Pacific Command during the

Vietnam War. All three men were graduates of the United States Naval Academy.

In 1967, McCain boarded the aircraft carrier USS *Forrestal* for a combat deployment to Vietnam. On July 29 of that year, a fire erupted aboard the carrier. McCain, who was in the cockpit of his A-4 jet, was caught in the middle of the blazing fire. After leaping from his plane, he rushed to the aid of a fellow aviator who was engulfed in a burning aircraft. As McCain struggled to pull the man to safety, a bomb from a nearby jet exploded, sending shrapnel into McCain's legs and chest. It took over twenty-four hours before the fire was extinguished. During that time 134 men died aboard the ship. It was the worst fire in U.S. naval history, but as often happens in disasters, valor and heroism were on full display.

After McCain recovered from his wounds, he immediately requested orders to another carrier deploying to Vietnam. He was assigned to the USS *Oriskany*. On October 26, 1967, while he was on his twenty-third bombing run over Hanoi, McCain's A-4 jet was hit by a surface-to-air missile. As the plane spun out of control, McCain pulled the ejection handle and was rocketed at high speed away from the jet. The velocity of the ejection broke both of his arms and fractured his leg. Landing in a nearby lake, he almost drowned before angry Vietnamese villagers pulled him ashore. Beaten and bayoneted by the mob, he was finally turned over to the North Vietnamese and taken to the infamous "Hanoi Hilton" POW camp.

Over the course of the next several months, McCain was interrogated, tortured, and given very little medical treatment. Moved to another camp and then thrown into solitary confinement, he seemed unlikely to survive. When the North Vietnamese finally realized he was the son of an American admiral, they decided to use him for propaganda. They would offer McCain early release from the POW camp, thereby showing his fellow POWs and the world that if you were privileged, the son of a Navy admiral, you got special treatment. Who in the world would have blamed McCain for leaving early? He had been beaten incessantly since arriving at the POW camp. Now was an opportunity to go home. Back to his family. Back to a comfortable life. Away from the hellhole he was living in. But Lieutenant Commander John McCain understood his duty to his fellow POWs and to his country. Article III of the military Code of Conduct says, "I will accept neither parole nor special favors from the enemy."

McCain refused repatriation. He would not violate the Code of Conduct. He would not desert his fellow POWs. *He would not fail to do his duty.* By refusing release, he inspired the other prisoners, he gave moral credence to the Code of Conduct, and he honored the legacy of every American ever captured. The North Vietnamese were furious, and for the next year McCain was tortured and brutalized weekly. Finally, five years later, five long years later, in March 1973, McCain and his fellow POWs were released.

———

Back in his Senate office, McCain and I talked about our time in the Navy. I told some stories from serving in Iraq and Afghanistan, and we laughed together as he recounted some amusing tales from his time as a Navy pilot. Although we came from different generations, we had a lot in common. Throughout the conversation he was gracious, funny, sometimes a bit irreverent, but it was clear to me that he had an undying gratitude for the men and women who served in the military. As I got up to leave, he shook my hand and held it tightly for a second or two. "I can't thank you enough for what you've done," he said. I didn't even know how to respond. Here was a man who had been to hell and back. A man who had shown the world what duty to the nation meant, *and he was thanking me*. I never forgot that moment and the humility of the man who served so well. The next day, I was recommended for confirmation by the Armed Services Committee and confirmed soon thereafter. Over the course of the next three years, I would see McCain many times. Some of those occasions were back in front of the Armed Services Committee, where his duty to the Senate and the American people was once again on full display.

———

Doing your duty need not require the sacrifice and valor of a John McCain. A few years earlier I was in Afghanistan when President Obama made a surprise visit to see Afghan president Hamid Karzai. After Air Force One landed at Bagram Air Base, the weather between Bagram and the capital city of Kabul turned bad and the president got stranded. That evening I got another powerful lesson in the value of doing your duty.

———

"Sir. The pilots say the mission is a no-go. There is only about one-hundred-foot visibility between here and Kabul and they're not going to risk flying POTUS in this weather."

"Roger," I answered. "Can't say I blame them."

"Yes sir. But what are they going to do with POTUS now? He's stuck in Bagram for the next six hours."

"Well, that's the Division Commander's responsibility. I'm sure the general will find something to keep the president busy."

I checked the operations schedule and our next mission wasn't going outside the wire for another two hours.

"I'm going to the gym for an hour," I said. "Let me know if anything changes."

"Roger, sir. I'll track you down."

I left the JOC, shifted into my PT gear, and jogged over to the large sprung shelter that served as our athletic facility. No sooner had I jumped on the treadmill than a young noncommissioned officer came bolting into the gym.

"Sir. We just received a call from the Division. They would like you to come over to the airfield and brief President Obama on our Afghan campaign plan."

"What? Now?"

"Yes sir. They have it scheduled in twenty minutes."

"Twenty minutes!" I said, looking at my watch. "All right. Grab Major Smith and tell him to print five copies of the campaign brief. I'll go change and meet you in the JOC in five minutes. Have the security guys ready to move."

Dashing out of the gym, I headed back to my room, changed, and ran up to the JOC. I checked my watch. We still had fifteen minutes to get to the airfield. Plenty of time, I thought. What could possibly go wrong driving five hundred yards to the airfield?

As the three-car convoy pulled up to my headquarters building, Pete Marlowe, my acting command sergeant major, jumped into the back left seat of the second car while I took my usual position behind the shotgun. I checked my watch again. Still ten minutes until showtime.

"Let's go, boys," Marlowe said, knowing I was anxious to get moving.

The driver floored the gas and we headed out from the camp. As expected, there was no traffic on the main street. In the distance, the lights of the airfield gave off an eerie yellow glow that illuminated the low-hanging clouds. A few hundred yards down the road, the lead car abruptly turned left into the back entrance of the airfield. Eight minutes till showtime. We were cutting it close.

There, standing at the gate, was a young female airman. As the convoy approached, she put out her hand, directing us to stop. Dressed in her battle fatigues, with an ill-fitting Kevlar helmet, oversized body armor, and carrying an M4 assault rifle, she seemed an unlikely candidate to be guarding the gate.

As the first vehicle came to a stop, my security officer, an Army sergeant, hopped out of the car and approached the young airman. I checked my watch again. Six minutes until I was supposed to brief the president of the United States.

Watching from the backseat, I could see the imposing figure of the sergeant leaning into the young airman. As he towered over the petite woman, he pointed his arm toward the airfield and I could hear him yelling above the sound of the vehicles. Now he was tapping his watch. Now he was yelling again. Now his arms were waving, and he was yelling, and he was tapping his watch. The woman refused to move. We still had time, I thought. I could almost see the hangar from where we were.

Seconds later the sergeant came back to my vehicle and Marlowe rolled down the window.

"Sir, she won't let us through," he said, gritting his teeth in anger. "She says she doesn't have authorization. I told her that she needs to get authorization ASAP! I told her that you have to brief the POTUS, now!"

Marlowe turned to me. "I got this, boss. Let me go talk with her."

I looked at my watch. Maybe we could still make it.

Marlowe got out of the car and slowly approached the young airman. I could hear his voice. It was calm and measured. He was explaining that I was a three-star admiral and that the president of the United States, the commander in chief, had asked for a briefing. So, could you please let us through, and we will explain to your boss that you did the right thing?

Nothing. She wouldn't move.

Before long I could hear yelling again. Hands pointing. Arms waving. Watches being tapped. I got out of the car.

Marlowe approached me. "Sir, she refuses to move. She said it's her responsibility to guard this gate and she has been told not to let anyone past. No one."

"Thanks. Let me see what I can do."

As I got closer to the young airman, I could see the fear in her eyes. My three stars were prominently displayed on the front of my shirt and on my hat.

"Good evening, Airman Jackson," I said, seeing the nametag on her uniform. "How are you?"

"Fine, sir," she said, coming to attention.

"Airman Jackson, I think my guys have told you, but I am supposed to be briefing the president, right this moment. And right now, we're running late."

"Yes sir. They told me." She was shaking a bit, but tried to calm herself.

"Look, Airman. You can see that I'm not a terrorist. I'm not Taliban. I'm an American naval officer who really needs to get on the flight line and over to see the president."

"Yes sir. I understand." Suddenly she stood up

a little straighter and looked me in the eye. "Sir. I know you have your job to do, but I have my job to do as well. I have the responsibility to guard this gate. And my orders are clear. No one is to enter without permission. And sir," she said, her voice quivering, "you don't have permission."

I checked my watch. We were now late. The president would be wondering where I was.

"Can you get permission?" I asked calmly.

"Sir, I'm working on it, but until my sergeant tells me that you're cleared, I can't let you through."

"Very well, Airman. I understand. Just let us know when we can continue."

I looked the young lady in the eye. Nothing was going to move her.

We waited a few more minutes as I wondered what I would say to the president. Finally, the young woman approached the lead car, informed them that she had received approval, and waved us through. As my car passed, she came to attention and saluted.

Over the next hour I briefed the president and

his team on the special operations missions that we were conducting across Afghanistan, Iraq, Yemen, and Somalia. The president never asked why I was late, and I never offered an explanation.

After the briefing, I returned to the waiting convoy and we headed back to my headquarters. As we passed the back gate, I asked the driver to pull over. Getting out of the car, I approached the young airman, who was still on duty. She came to attention.

"Airman Jackson," I said, raising my voice. "I just want you to know that I was ten minutes late to brief the president of the United States. Ten minutes!"

She didn't say a word.

"I was late because you refused to let me through. You wouldn't let me through when my sergeant asked. You wouldn't let me through when my command sergeant major asked. And you wouldn't even let me through when I asked, and I'm a damn three-star admiral!"

"Yes sir," she said quietly, looking down at her shoes.

Reaching into my pocket, I pulled out my Command Challenge Coin, given only to those soldiers who do exceptional work.

I smiled and placed the coin in the airman's right hand.

"You did exactly what you were supposed to do. You can come work for me anytime."

She looked down at the coin, looked at me, down at the coin, and then she smiled.

"I was just doing my duty, sir."

"Exactly right."

———

General Order Number One is the foundation of the United States military. What it says is important, but what it means is the key to a life well lived and a healthy society. It says, "I will take charge of my post and all government property in view." It means that you are responsible for your actions and the actions that affect the things around you. The airman was responsible for her gate. She was not blindly following orders. She understood that the safety of the president might be at risk if she failed to obey those orders. Somewhere on the flight line a sergeant was responsible for several airmen. Somewhere else a captain was responsible for several sergeants; a colonel was responsible for several captains; and a general was responsible for several colonels. All those people performing their duties allowed for the safe visit of the president of the United States. General Order Number One is about your duty, your responsibility to the men and women who work with you, for you, and for whom you work.

———

In the course of my long military career I saw remarkable young Americans perform their duty at every level, under every conceivable condition. I remember the nineteen-year-old administrative clerk who thought his job was unimportant. How could filing veterans' benefits compare to the warriors who were going outside the wire every day? It wasn't until he received a note of thanks from the wife of a fallen soldier that he realized his seemingly mundane job was really quite important. Or the Army supply sergeant who worked forty-eight hours straight just to get a Thanksgiving turkey to a Special Forces unit that hadn't seen real food in months. In Kandahar, Afghanistan, I recall the Air Force nurse who refused to leave her patient in the operating room when enemy rockets started falling around the hospital. I can't forget the medevac pilots who flew into a raging firefight to extract two of my fellow SEALs. Or the two Marines in Ramadi, Iraq, who stood their ground when a large vehicle-borne IED raced toward their post. They did their duty and saved the lives of 150 Iraqis and Americans. I also remember the hundreds of foreign service officers, intelligence professionals, and law enforcement agents who all did their duty so that others might live.

There is an old proverb, "For want of a nail, the shoe was lost. For want of a shoe, the horse was lost. For want of a horse, the knight was lost. For want of the knight, the battle was lost. For want of a battle, the kingdom was lost. The kingdom was lost for the want of a nail." There are many interpretations of this old saying, but to me it epitomizes doing your duty. If the blacksmith had done his duty and placed the nail in the horseshoe correctly, the kingdom would not have been lost. If the clerk doesn't do the paperwork, or the sergeant doesn't deliver the chow, or the nurse, the pilot, or the Marines don't do their duty, the kingdom is always at risk.

The idea of duty is a simple one. We all have a job to do in life. Whether that job is serving customers in a restaurant, taking care of our family, teaching our children, policing our cities, caring for the ill and infirm, protecting our gate, following the military Code of Conduct, or leading the country, we must do our job to the best of our ability. We must do our job well, not because it serves our interests, but because it serves the interests of others. We do not live in this world alone. Duty is a recognition that you have a responsibility to your fellow man and woman. It is an unselfish act, whether great or small, that contributes to the welfare of humanity. That is what makes it so very powerful. *If you want to be a hero, it's easy. Just do your duty!*

The Hero Code

Whatever job I am given, whatever duty I am bound by, I will do it to the best of my ability.

CHAPTER EIGHT

Hope

"To live without hope is to cease to live."

—FYODOR DOSTOEVSKY

There was a slight whiff of rubbing alcohol in the air as I walked past the infusion center in the MD Anderson Cancer Center. A dozen or so people were lying in hospital beds as a two-liter bag dripped lifesaving drugs into their veins. Most had lost their hair or had that exhausted look from the long fight. I tried to remain calm as I approached the waiting room.

Two months earlier, while serving in Afghanistan, I received a video call from a doctor at my home base in North Carolina. She informed me that my recent bone marrow biopsy determined that I had chronic lymphocytic leukemia (CLL). Her prognosis was not encouraging. She told me that the CLL was in my spleen. Consequently, I would have to return immediately from Afghanistan, have my spleen removed, and begin chemotherapy. With zero fanfare, she also said that my career was likely over, as I would have to devote so much of my time to fighting this disease. I was stunned by the diagnosis and struggled to get through the early days after the call. Soon thereafter, I returned to North Carolina and informed Georgeann. Like every great partner, she immediately started looking for solutions. Within hours she identified the world's foremost expert in CLL, Dr. Michael Keating. As it so happened, he was at MD Anderson in my home state of Texas.

As we sat waiting in the doctor's office, I wondered how my life would change. In my mind, I went through all the worst-case scenarios. Twenty years earlier, my mother had passed away from lung cancer and I remembered being at her bedside in the last moments. She wasn't conscious and the cancer had left her thin and ghostly pale. It was gut-wrenching to watch her take her final breath. I could envision my kids at my bedside, and I didn't want them to go through the same pain.

As these frightening thoughts tumbled through

my brain, the door to the small office swung open and a large ruddy-faced man barged in. I immediately hopped up from my chair. Dressed in a white lab coat with a clipboard in one hand, he quickly surveyed the room. Tossing the clipboard on the desk, he walked up to me and in a thick Australian accent yelled, "Give me a hug!" Before I could object, he wrapped his big arms around me and squeezed me tightly.

Turning to Georgeann, he said, "So you must be the wife?"

Georgeann nodded.

"Well, you can stop looking for a new boyfriend. He's going to be fine."

Georgeann and I stared at each other, stunned by this revelation.

"I'm sorry, Doctor," I stammered. "What'd you say?"

Picking up the clipboard, Keating grinned. "I said you're going to be just fine."

"Okay..." I replied, somewhat in disbelief. "My

doctor in North Carolina said that I was going to have to have my spleen removed and start immediately on chemotherapy."

"Nah," he said, turning to face me. "We have some better options now."

Before I could continue, he turned to Georgeann. "What do you think? Do you want to keep him around for a little longer?"

Georgeann hadn't said a word since he burst through the door. I could see the tears welling up in her eyes.

"Yes," she said quietly, turning to look at me.

"Yeah, he seems like the kind of guy you might want to keep around," he roared.

Over the next few minutes, Keating walked us through the results of the lab work, carefully explaining what each number meant and how the CLL was affecting my body. We covered all the possible therapeutic protocols and the timeline for treatment. While my initial diagnosis in North Carolina was correct, Keating and his colleagues had developed new therapeutics for dealing with the CLL. Throughout the discussion, he laughed and told some jokes and several tales from his childhood in Australia. By the end of the conversation, all the anxiety I had was gone.

"What questions do you have?" Keating asked Georgeann.

"Well…" She paused, looking at me again. "Should he eat more fruits and vegetables?"

Keating smiled and shook his head. "Nah."

"Well…" She thought again. "Should he get more exercise?"

Keating looked me over and shook his head again. "He looks to be in great shape to me."

"Well, should he cut back on his alcohol?"

Keating abruptly rose from his chair, a feigned look of disgust on his face. "Oh God, no!" he shouted.

All three of us started to laugh.

I quickly jumped into the discussion. "Then can I go back to Afghanistan?"

"Sure," he said. "Just try not to get shot."

All of a sudden, my life had been given back to me. I could see a different future. *I had hope*. Instead of focusing on all the bad that might come my way, I looked forward to the wonderful possibilities in the years ahead. I wasn't naïve to the eventual outcome of the disease. CLL affects your immune system, weakening your body and making it susceptible to other cancers and other diseases. But somehow this boisterous old Australian emboldened me to be optimistic: to smile, to laugh, to tell a joke or two, to live life to its fullest and not spend all my time worrying about what might be. When "what might be" became "what is"—we would deal with it then. His optimism was contagious. His hopefulness released me from the burden of fear. He gave me the strength to carry on. Every six months from that day forward, I returned to MD Anderson and refilled my tank of optimism, recharged my sense of hope.

Over the course of the next four years, I would

continue to lead special operations forces around the world. In 2011, the troops under my command brought justice to Osama bin Laden. From 2011 to 2014, I commanded all of U.S. Special Operations. I retired in 2014, and in the three years following my retirement I was honored to be the chancellor of the University of Texas System. Finally, in 2017, the CLL caught up to me, as I suffered from severe anemia and a drastically low platelet count. Dr. Keating, still quick with a good joke and a hearty laugh, pumped me full of some lifesaving chemicals and made me well again.

I found in my travels around the world that hope is the strongest force in the universe. With hope you can endure anything. Without it, you are destined to a life of fear and despair. But rarely have I seen the power of hope so clearly manifested as when I had the opportunity to meet with former POWs from the Vietnam War.

———

During the Vietnam War, over a thousand Americans were taken prisoner. Their treatment at the hands of the North Vietnamese was barbaric. Imprisoned for years, they were beaten, isolated, and at times deprived of food and water. With each passing year their hope for liberation faded. Most believed they would never see their families again. All they had was each other.

In 1970, an Army Special Forces unit, the Green Berets, conducted a rescue operation into North Vietnam to free some of the POWs located at a camp called Son Tay. Intelligence revealed that over sixty American POWs were held prisoner at the camp and that their treatment was so brutal that quick action was required. On November 21, the Green Berets boarded six helicopters and flew 680 miles from Thailand into Laos and finally crossed the border into North Vietnam. When they landed at the camp, they immediately took fire from the North Vietnamese guards. After an intense firefight that left forty-two enemy killed, it became painfully clear that the POWs had been moved. Intelligence would later show that the North Vietnamese had relocated the Americans months earlier because of a contaminated water supply. The rescue operation was a complete failure. Or so the soldiers thought. It wasn't until two years later, when the American POWs were released, that the full impact of the raid was understood.

In April 1973, Texas billionaire Ross Perot graciously hosted all the POWs, the Son Tay Raiders, and their families at a reunion in San Francisco. For years the Son Tay Raiders had anguished over the failure of the mission. But the POWs had a different tale to tell.

"We knew we hadn't been forgotten," one POW said, his eyes filling with tears.

"The raid did so very much for our morale," another offered.

"The Raiders gave us hope, and from that day on we knew we could endure whatever trials came our way," was a familiar refrain.

They gave us hope.

Every year since 1973, with the support of the Perot family, the Son Tay Raiders, the former POWs, and all their families meet to pay their respects to the fallen, to honor those who sacrificed their freedom for the nation, and to thank those who tried to save them. I was fortunate to join them in 2005, and those who were imprisoned never forgot that feeling of hope. The raid and the hope that it inspired lifted the spirits of every American held in Vietnam and sustained them through their darkest hours.

———

What is hope but a belief that tomorrow will be better: that tomorrow your children will be happier; that tomorrow your cancer will be in remission; that tomorrow your rescuers will try again; that tomorrow your country will not be at war; that tomorrow the nation will be united and the world will be safer? But hope is more than just a fanciful wish. If you want to bring hope to the world, you will have to find what you're good at and give it to others. People believe in the hope-givers, the Dr. Keatings and the Green Berets, *only* if they believe they can deliver on their promise. The good news is, *each of us has something that we are good at*—something we can give to others that makes them hopeful. A talent that someone else in the world is lacking. We are faster, stronger, smarter, kinder, gentler, richer, more courageous, more forgiving, more gracious, more trustworthy, more honest, more of something. All heroes have something that makes them unique. Find that talent and use it to inspire others—to give hope, to make tomorrow a better day.

The Hero Code

I will use my unique talents to inspire others and give them hope that tomorrow will be a better day.

CHAPTER NINE

Humor

---✶---

"Humor is mankind's greatest blessing."

—MARK TWAIN

B ased in the resort town of Coronado, California, Underwater Demolition Team Eleven (UDT-11) was one of the three UDT/SEAL Teams on the West Coast in the late 1970s. Their facility was a collection of World War II–era buildings situated just fifty yards off the beach. No matter where you were inside the compound, the smell of the Pacific Ocean and wet suits drying on the line was always in the air. To me, it was the smell of adventure. Somewhere Navy frogmen were locking out of submarines, jumping out of airplanes, blowing things up, and preparing for the next great battle or covert operation. Each of the three Teams had its own dive locker, armory, parachute loft, and locker room. Most of the 150 sailors who formed UDT-11 were highly decorated Vietnam veterans. Every gathering of more than two men resulted in stories of missions, both victorious and disastrous, that found a place in UDT lore. But as a young frogman just out of training, nothing shaped my SEAL character quite like morning physical training (PT) on the Grinder. The Grinder was a rough patch of asphalt where Navy SEALs started each day. The asphalt grinds you down physically, tests your desire to succeed, and challenges your humility. On the Grinder, great lessons in life are learned.

"So, you're the new guy?" one of my officers remarked.

"Yes sir," I responded. It's my first day in the Teams."

"First day in the Teams? Well, you're going to love it here," he said. "The guys will welcome you with open arms. The old Vietnam vets are really nice. They love officers. Particularly new officers. They'll treat you really well."

"Great. I'm looking forward to it."

A sly grin came across the officer's face.

Dressed in khaki swim trunks, blue-and-gold T-shirts, and jungle boots, we headed out of the building and onto the Grinder. After a short daily briefing from the executive officer we broke ranks and formed up into a circle. The PT Circle.

And then it began.

"So, Ensign. I understand you went to Texas A&M."

"No, Chief. The University of Texas. Not A&M."

"So you couldn't get into a real school?"

Before I could answer, someone offered a response. "He's from Texas. There aren't any real schools in Texas."

"So you weren't smart enough to get into the Academy?"

"We frogmen expect our officers to be smart. What did you major in?"

I hesitated. "Journalism, Chief."

"Journalism! You're a damn reporter! Hey, XO, we don't need no damn reporter in our ranks."

The executive officer smiled, but said nothing.

"What SEAL training class were you in?" a man at the far end of the circle shouted.

"Class 95," I yelled back.

"You've got to be kidding me!" an older officer said, spitting out a wad of tobacco.

"I heard Class 95 was the easiest class ever. They had a summer Hell Week."

Over the next fifteen minutes all fifty men in the circle had something to say about my shortfalls. In between repetitions of push-ups, flutter kicks, sit-ups, and burpees, they questioned my parentage, my athleticism, my intellect, my state of origin, the quality of my SEAL training class, and of course, my love life.

"You got a girlfriend?" one of the salty old chiefs asked.

"I do, Chief."

"What's she look like?"

"Oh, she's pretty. Very petite. Brown hair, hazel eyes, about five foot four."

The chief smiled. "Do you think she'd like a swarthy Italian with a mustache?" he said, twirling the ends of his long handlebar.

I saw an opening.

"No, Chief," I said, looking around the Grinder. "She likes men that are taller than she is."

The circle went quiet. The chief, who stood no taller than five foot four, got up off the Grinder and walked up to where I was standing. Inches from my face, he sneered at me and said, "Are you calling me short?"

The men in the circle were shaking their heads. One mouthed, "Don't go there, Ensign." Another said softly, "He's very sensitive about his height."

"Well, Chief, you are looking up at me."

Everyone on the Grinder stopped exercising and turned my way.

"What! Do you think that's funny, Ensign? Do you think insulting a chief petty officer in the

United States Navy is funny? I am very, very sensitive about my height, and that hurts me."

I paused, wondering whether I had taken my repartee too far.

Suddenly, the chief burst out laughing, and the rest of the men in the circle joined him.

"Welcome to the Teams, Ensign!"

When the physical training ended, the chief and all the other members of the Team came by to shake my hand and welcome me to UDT-11. I had passed the test. I had a sense of humor.

Life on the Grinder was a daily reminder of the value of humor. No matter who you were, from the commanding officer down to the lowest seaman, you were subject to being publicly and good-naturedly ridiculed. The daily roastings kept you humble when your vanity exceeded your success. The pointed barbs put things in perspective when you took your failures too seriously. The back-and-forth banter sharpened your wits so that you could answer an attack with a cutting retort, a retort that always got a chuckle but never truly offended.

In the SEAL Teams nothing seemed beyond the scope of a good laugh. Every day some jokester was setting you up for a hilarious fall: having you return an important call from the commander, one that he never made; switching out your wet suit for one two sizes too small; having a woman show up at work claiming to be your ex-wife; putting the entire Team's drinks on your bar tab; conducting an emergency midnight recall, in which you found that you were the only one there. Every prank was meant to humble you, but at the same time it was meant to boost the morale of the Team. If you handled it well, you were respected for your humility. If you chafed at the joke and sought petty revenge, you could easily lose the locker room. Accepting the humor of the moment made you stronger in almost every regard.

Years after UDT-11, I was on a training mission

in Egypt. After we inserted the SEAL Team for their operation, the engine on my small boat conked out and me and my crew were adrift at sea for ten hours. Eventually, an Egyptian Coast Guard vessel arrived and we had to be unceremoniously towed back into Alexandria. It was a terribly embarrassing scene. But as my boat pulled back into the harbor, my SEAL teammates were waiting for me. Knowing how humiliating the moment was, one would have assumed a more dignified welcome. Instead they all lined up on the pier and sang the theme from the old TV show *Gilligan's Island*: *"Just sit right back and you'll hear a tale, a tale of a fateful trip..."* They held a sign that read "Welcome Back SS Minnow."

Or four years later when a parachute accident almost took my life, the Team had T-shirts made with a cartoon of me parachuting with an anvil tied to my back.

Or three years after that when the entire senior staff of the Joint Special Operations Command, led by General Stan McChrystal, roasted me for an hour on a videoconference, once again highlighting my many shortfalls: "Calling McRaven the smartest SEAL in the Teams is like saying he's the fastest sumo wrestler in a race. What good is he? He's a Texan who can't ride a horse and a Navy guy who can't sail a boat. Basketball? The man's got a two-inch vertical leap."

There were many more salacious barbs, all in good fun, that had me roaring with laughter. Rarely had I felt so respected by the men I served with.

Never was a sense of humor more apparent than in the hundreds of soldiers I visited in the hospitals in Iraq, Afghanistan, and stateside. Each one had their story: a firefight, an IED, a rocket, a mortar. Something horrific had devastated their life, but they refused to give in to pity. They would fight their fear and the uncertainty with laughter.

I recall the Army sergeant who had been the gunner on a Humvee when the vehicle was hit by an RPG. In the ICU, his wounds were gruesome. The blast left him severely burned, and his body had swelled, stretching the skin to its breaking point. But I could see in his eyes that he was a fighter. And a man with a sense of humor. When I joked that he looked like crap, he quickly responded, "Oh, but sir, you should see the other guy." It was a standard punch line. A give-and-take between warriors. The joke was a shield protecting him from the seriousness of his injuries and a sword that struck out at the enemy, saying, *You didn't defeat me because I can still laugh.*

I can remember the double amputee who had been five foot five before he lost his legs but now stood six foot two with the new prosthetics. He used to brag that the extra height made him more attractive to women. Or the one-handed Ranger who joked that with his mechanical vise grip he could finally hold a golf club correctly. The best soldiers, the toughest of the lot, knew how to use humor to deflect the pain of their loss.

But no pain was more agonizing than the loss of a fellow soldier. I was honored to attend dozens of memorial services, opportunities to recognize the remarkable heroism of a fallen warrior. Without exception, the soldiers who eulogized their comrades used humor to lessen the pain, to show that their friend's life, no matter how it ended, had been filled with fun and laughter. Every fallen hero had a bit of prankster in them. I recall a SEAL who filled his buddy's wet suit with Bengay; a Ranger who added extra weight to his friend's rucksack during a long training march; a Green Beret who pretended his fellow jumper's parachute was mispacked; and a helo pilot who sent his wingman to the wrong ship during an exercise. Every fallen hero had also been on the receiving end of an equally funny joke. Those powerful eulogies made it clear that as sad as the loss might be and as bitter as the end may seem, if the hero's life was filled with laughter, then a good life it had been.

———

In the midst of the American Civil War, President Abraham Lincoln was known for his sense of humor. Here was a man who had been defeated in every election before president, who suffered from depression, who lost two children at young ages, and who now bore the burden of a war that was destroying the Union, and he constantly resorted to humor.

He joked so often that he was criticized for not taking the battle losses seriously enough, but Lincoln understood the value of humor. He used humor to soften the blows of defeat, to assuage an angry constituent, to mollify feuding generals, and to bolster the morale of the Union.

Most of his jokes were aimed inward. He loved to tell the story of a man who approached him on a train one day. The man said, "I have an article in my possession which belongs to you." Taking a jack-knife from his pocket, the man explained, "This knife was placed in my hands with the promise that I was to keep it until I found a man uglier than myself. Allow me now to say, sir, that I think you are fairly entitled to the property."

A reporter from the *New York Herald* once wrote, "I think it would be hard to find one who tells better jokes, enjoys them better and laughs more often than Abraham Lincoln." Lincoln so valued a good joke that he reportedly believed that young children should be taught humor in school right along with reading, writing, and arithmetic. In times of upheaval, crisis, and turmoil, great leaders turn to humor as a source of strength for themselves and those that they lead.

———

Humor is one of the most important qualities for any hero. If you want to show courage, laugh in the face of danger. If you want to show humility, laugh at yourself. If you want to sacrifice, sacrifice your vanity for a joke. If you want to be compassionate, let humor soften the blow of the pain. If you want to be honest, chuckle at your shortcomings. If you want to give hope, use humor to lighten the darkness. If you want to persevere through tough times, you had better learn to laugh. Find your comedic voice and use your wit to save those around you, to free them from their sorrow, to give them joy, and to help them see the humor in the darkest of times. *This is what real heroes do.*

The Hero Code

I will use humor to comfort others, and never be afraid to laugh at myself.

CHAPTER TEN

Forgiveness

"The weak can never forgive, forgiveness is the attribute of the strong."

—MAHATMA GANDHI

I sat cross-legged on the floor of the large room, surrounded by a hundred or so Afghans from the village of Gardez. Outside the building, several hundred more had gathered to witness the event. Across from me was an old man, dressed in a traditional white cotton shalwar kameez, with its long flowing top and baggy trousers. His brown face was drawn with grief and weathered with time. Next to him was his oldest son, younger by twenty years and clad in all black. The anger on his face was apparent. And who could blame him?

Weeks before, a mission to capture a Taliban target in Gardez had gone terribly wrong. Soldiers from my unit had surrounded the old man's compound, hoping to capture a local Taliban leader. Two of the man's sons, seeing the soldiers on their roof, but thinking *they* were Taliban, tried to defend themselves. The Americans fired at the men, assuming they were enemy sympathizers, and the two sons were killed in the fight. The old man's daughter and two other women were also killed when one soldier's errant rounds went through a door and struck them. In all my time in the military, it was the most gut-wrenching tragedy I had faced.

In accordance with Afghan tradition, I came that day to offer reparations in the form of several sheep and some modest compensation. But the real reason I went to Gardez was to apologize, to let the father know that I was truly sorry for the pain my soldiers and this war had caused him. I had no idea how the old man could forgive me. Had it been me, the hatred would have been too deep to reconcile with anyone even remotely responsible for my children's death.

A middle-aged man with a long brown beard, who I assumed was an imam, acted as moderator and translator. The father, his eyes cast down in sadness, could barely look up from the floor. Finally, after a long introduction, the imam turned to me. What could I say to ease the old man's pain and to convince him that I was sincere in my regret and my apology was heartfelt? What could possibly make up for such a tragic act of war? I had thought long and hard about what I would say. Before leaving my home base at Bagram I consulted with my Afghan counterpart, General Salam. When I asked Salam what I should say to the father and how I should express my sorrow, he seemed perplexed by my question.

"The father will forgive you," Salam said very matter-of-factly.

"How is that possible?" I said in disbelief.

Salam craned his neck as if he was still trying to grasp my question.

"It is what Allah would want."

Somewhat exasperated, I said, "Yes, of course, Salam, but not all Muslims I have met are so forgiving."

Salam smiled, understanding the not-so-veiled reference to Al Qaeda and the Taliban.

"I know this village. They are good people. Good Muslims. The father will forgive you."

Salam could see the skeptical look on my face.

"The Quran teaches us the value of mercy. The father will forgive you because it will take away his burden. Not the burden of his loss. Nothing can ever take that away. But the burden of his hatred and anger. Forgiveness is a great gift not only to those that receive it, but to those that give it."

Sitting there in the long hall, I thought back on Salam's words. Could it be so?

I looked first at the son. His eyes narrowed and his brow furrowed. He clearly wanted me dead. Then I cast my eyes on the father.

Taking a deep breath, I said, "I am the commander of the soldiers who accidentally killed your loved ones. I came here today to give my condolences to you and to your family and to your friends."

I paused, waiting for the imam to translate my words. The father never looked up. I continued.

"I also came today to ask your forgiveness for these terrible tragedies."

Finally, the father raised his head and looked me in the eye. His face was expressionless, but his eyes were kind. Deep, sad, heartbroken, but kind. He nodded for me to continue.

"Sir, you and I are different. You are a family man, living at home with many children and many friends. I am a soldier who has spent most of my life overseas away from my family. But I have children as well and my heart grieves for you."

Tears began to well up in the old man's eyes.

"But we have one thing in common, one very important thing," I said. "We both believe in a God who shows great love and compassion. I pray for you today, sir, that in your grief he will show you love and compassion and ease your pain. I also pray today that he will show mercy on me and my men for this awful tragedy."

Looking at the father and the son, I could barely continue to talk. I couldn't even imagine their pain.

The father nodded slightly. Once again, I asked for their forgiveness.

The son leaned over to the father and whispered something in his ear. The look of anger on the son's face had softened. The fire in his eyes was gone. The son spoke for the father, and the imam translated.

"Thank you very much," the son said. "We will not keep anything in our heart against you."

We will not keep anything in our heart against you. That is the essence of forgiveness. As I left the village of Gardez that day, I felt a burden had been lifted, but more importantly, I had a renewed sense of forgiveness. I prayed that the time would come when I could be as merciful to someone else as the father had been to me. I hoped someday I could be as good a man as he was.

———

When Dylann Roof, the white supremacist who killed nine parishioners at the Emanuel AME Church in Charleston, South Carolina, stood before the court, the families of the victims each took a turn forgiving Roof for his heinous and incomprehensible crime.

"I forgive you and have mercy on your soul," they said.

They refused to let Roof's anger be their burden.

André Comte-Sponville, a professor of philosophy at the Sorbonne in Paris, writes, "The point [of forgiveness] is to overcome our own hatred if we cannot make him overcome his; to achieve self-mastery if we cannot master him; to win at least this victory over evil and hatred and not add evil to evil; to avoid becoming his accomplice as well as his victim."

G. K. Chesterton, the great English writer, philosopher and theologian, once wrote that, "To love means loving the unlovable. To forgive means pardoning the unpardonable." Dylann Roof's actions were unpardonable, but the families would not become Roof's accomplices in this vile act of hatred. They were the victors, not the victims.

However, not every act of forgiveness need be predicated on something so loathsome. Society today seems to be easily offended. We are quick to anger, and some people believe every offensive act, no matter the intent, requires a swift rebuke. The hardest thing any hero can do is to forgive. It is easier to storm the hill, fight the fire, and stop a madman with a gun. It is hard to forgive, because we are afraid. Afraid that forgiving will take away the anger that drives us, the hatred that motivates us, the righteous indignation of being wronged. We want more than anything to harness the outrage, feel the power of injustice, and the fury of discontent, so we can lash out at the offender and feel justified. We think that retribution, no matter how small or how large, will soothe our soul.

It will not.

As Christ hung nailed to the cross, scourged

and dying, he looked up to heaven and said, "Father, forgive them, for they know not what they do."

Forgiveness will never be easy. It was not meant to be. It takes a strong person to forgive. But the act of forgiving will strengthen your character immeasurably and it will rid you of hatred that is the demise of so many good men and women.

Be the victor, not the victim.

Learn to forgive.

The Hero Code

No matter how great or small
the offense against me, I will
try to forgive. I will be the victor,
not the victim.

EPILOGUE

As I entered the conference room and took my seat at the head of the table, I wondered how different my new life would be. After thirty-seven years in the Navy, I had exchanged my uniform for a suit. Now I was the chancellor of the University of Texas System, overseeing eight universities, six academic health care institutions, 230,000 students, and 100,000 employees. The other executives sitting around the table didn't look like my SEALs and soldiers. Dressed in business attire, they were educators, doctors, lawyers, and former university presidents. The students, faculty, and researchers I met prior to taking the job seemed less disciplined than my Rangers and Green Berets. The alumni, the civic leaders, and the legislators whom I encountered during my transition were good folks, but in my heart, I knew they were different than the warriors with whom I had served. I had so loved being with the soldiers, sailors, airmen, Marines, and civil servants, and I worried that I would never again find men and women of such character; that I would never again see the courage, the humility, the sacrifice, or the sense of duty that I experienced in the service. But as it turned out, there was no need to worry. *There are heroes everywhere.*

There are heroes in the classrooms educating the youth of America and teaching them to be better citizens.

There are heroes caring for the sick and dying in hospitals across the nation.

There are heroes keeping our streets safe from violence and crime.

There are heroes working the farms and the ranches to put food on the table.

There are heroes speaking out against injustice and racism.

There are heroes in the halls of the state capitols enacting laws to help the underprivileged and downtrodden.

There are heroes in the homes across Texas and every other state working hard to make a better life for their children.

And when tragedy struck during Hurricane Harvey, when we were engulfed in the pandemic crisis, and when the upheaval of social injustice poured out into the streets, those same heroes rose to the occasion. The qualities we admire so much shone through and illuminated our path forward.

———

The Hero Code is not some impossible set of values that none of us can attain. On the contrary, most of the heroes I have met and most of the heroes in this book were just common people before they were thrust into the crucible of action. Ashley White was just a young woman from Ohio doing her job in the Army, but her legacy of courage will be forever remembered by the soldiers with whom she served. Ralph Johnson was a poor black teenager raised in the South, with little promise of greatness, until he sacrificed his life for his fellow Marines. John Adams was a young lawyer of no particular fame when he defended the British redcoats and changed the course of the American judicial system. The people of North Platte, Nebraska, were just being kind when they served the soldiers heading to war, never knowing that their compassion would alter the lives of so many young men. Dr. Jim Allison was raised in a small town in Texas, and his only virtues seemed to be his curiosity and his dogged persistence. Nothing about him seemed destined for scientific immortality.

What set these people apart was that their character had been molded over time, shaped by a caring parent, a loving teacher, a demanding coach, a compassionate policeman, a forgiving clergyman, an inspiring soldier, or a friend with a great sense of humor. Through study, reflection, and experience they learned to be courageous, to be humble, to sacrifice for others, to be men and women of integrity, to show compassion for others, to persevere through the difficult times, to give people hope, to do their duty no matter how mundane it might seem, to laugh through the darkness, and to forgive those who do them wrong. Being a hero is a learned experience.

Lincoln once said that "I will prepare and someday my chance will come." Well, someday your chance may come to be a hero. Someday a small act of compassion may change the course of one person's life. Someday a small act of courage may change the course of a nation, and someday a small act of sacrifice may change the course of history. You must start preparing now by learning from the heroes that came before you and those who walk among you today.

Being a hero won't be easy. It wasn't meant to be. Being a hero can be filled with pain and disappointment. It is dangerous at times. If you stand your ground or stand up for what you believe in, you are likely to suffer the "slings and arrows of outrageous fortune." But we call people heroes for a reason. Their actions rise above the crowd. They separate themselves from the weak-kneed, the bench-sitters, those who lack the moral fortitude to do the right thing, and, in the end, the heroes make us better people, a better society, and a better world. As much as I hoped the Man of Steel would be around to save the world, he is not. It is up to us. *It is up to you.*

Be the hero we need
you to be—live the Hero Code.

THE HERO CODE

1. I will always strive to be COURAGEOUS; to take one step forward as I confront my fears.

2. I will work to be HUMBLE; to recognize the limits of my intellect, my understanding, and my power.

3. I will learn to SACRIFICE by giving a little of my time, my talent, and my treasure to those in need.

4. I will be a person of INTEGRITY; every decision I make and every action I take will be moral, legal, and ethical.

5. I will be kind and COMPASSIONATE to at least one person every single day and expect nothing in return.

6. I will never give up on matters that are important to me, my family, my country, or my faith. I will PERSEVERE.

7. Whatever job I am given, whatever DUTY I am bound by, I will do it to the best of my ability.

8. I will use my unique talents to inspire others and give them HOPE that tomorrow will be a better day.

9. I will use HUMOR to comfort others, and never be afraid to laugh at myself.

10. No matter how great or small the offense against me, I will try to FORGIVE. I will be the victor, not the victim.

ACKNOWLEDGMENTS

I would like to thank Rachel Kambury and Sean Desmond at Hachette for both their friendship and their encouragement in writing this book. As always, none of this would have been possible without the assistance of my friend and lawyer, Mr. Bob Barnett. You are the best in the business. Finally, I am blessed to have the finest "first reader" imaginable—my wife, Georgeann. Her thoroughness, candor, and tough love were critical in ensuring the book was at its best. My thanks to all of you.

ABOUT THE AUTHOR

Admiral William H. McRaven, U.S. Navy (Retired) is the #1 *New York Times* bestselling author of *Make Your Bed* and the *New York Times* bestseller *Sea Stories: My Life in Special Operations*. In his thirty-seven years as a Navy SEAL, he commanded at every level. As a Four-Star Admiral, his final assignment was as Commander of all U.S. Special Operations Forces. After retiring from the Navy, he served as the Chancellor of the University of Texas System from 2015 to 2018. He now lives in Austin, Texas, with his wife, Georgeann.